MY
FRIEND
HAS
FOUR
PARENTS

MY FRIEND HAS FOUR PARENTS

MARGARET O. HYDE

McGRAW-HILL BOOK COMPANY
New York · St. Louis · San Francisco
· Bogotá · Düsseldorf · Madrid · Mexico · Montreal
· New Delhi · Panama · Paris · São Paulo
· Singapore · Tokyo · Toronto

LIBRARY OF CONGRESS IN PUBLICATION DATA

Hyde; Maragret Oldroyd,
My friend has four parents.

Summary: Examines various situations that arise
from divorce and remarriage, including one-parent
families, "stepfamilies," and living part-time with
both parents. Also includes information on custody,
parental kidnapping, and sources of outside help.
1. Divorce—United States—Juvenile literature.
2. Remarriage—United States—Juvenile literature.
3. Stepparents—United States—Juvenile literature.
[1. Divorce. 2. Remarriage. 3. Stepparents]

I. Title.
HQ834.H93   306.8'7   81-1533
ISBN 0-07-031644-9   AACR2

CONTENTS

1

PARENTS DIVIDED AND MULTIPLIED

Can you imagine having four parents, eight grandparents, and five stepbrothers and stepsisters? This is true for some children whose parents have been divorced and have remarried. Such families have been given many names, such as the extended family, stepfamily, blended family, reconstituted family, meta family, and conjugal continuation.

Perhaps you or some of your friends have more than two parents. Perhaps you live with just one parent. Families in which parents differ from the original two have become quite common today. Estimates of the number of children who live in such families vary a great deal, but all run in the millions.

In the United States alone there are probably about seven million children under the age of eighteen who live in a household with a stepparent, and there are at least fifteen million children who live with a stepparent part of the time. The incidence of stepfamilies is estimated to be between 10 and 15 percent of all households in the United States. These families experience unique problems in addition to those common to all families. Almost all families have disagreements about things such as household responsibilities, finances, discipline, and communication between adolescents and adults. Living in step may be especially difficult since the stepfamily has many qualities that place additional emotional burdens on its members. For example, there may be feelings of conflicting loyalties, of unexpected resentment, of disappointment with hopes that don't come true, and feelings of not belonging. However, a National Institute of Health-funded investigation found that stepchildren view their own mental health to be as good as that of other children. This study also found that stepchildren were as successful at achieving as other children. On the other hand, there are studies that do not agree with these evaluations.

No one knows how many children live with just one parent. It is estimated that more than three million children are currently growing up in fatherless homes in the United States. The percentage of children under the age of six living in fatherless homes is estimated to be the same as that of children with two parents present. Two-thirds of the children born to unmarried mothers are not adopted, but are reared in one-parent homes, foster homes, and institutions. Certainly, the children who live with just one parent can find many friends with whom to share their feelings.

Living in a one-parent home can have special problems, too. The feelings of abandonment, sadness, guilt about being the cause of divorce, and other problems are described in this book. Children who have lost a parent through death are especially vulnerable to feelings of guilt and abandonment. They may be afraid to love again because they feel they would not be so miserable now if they had not loved the dead parent so much. Perhaps, they feel, it is better not to love at all. Some children even blame the remaining parent who is left to carry on for the death of the missing parent. These are just some of the problems that confront children in a single-parent home, but the forecast for their future need not be gloomy.

Even though each family situation is unique, there are many problems that are common to children who live in families with other than their two biological parents. The examples in the following pages may help you and your friends to live more comfortably with parents divided and multiplied. Some of the ways of working through problems may be useful to you and friends who are challenged by such problems.

No matter how many people are part of your family and no matter how they are related to you, your family is still the place to go when you feel the need for intimacy. The family is the source of emotional support for its members even though the members may be changing. The traditional relationships that evolve slowly in the original family may never be replaced when parents divorce and remarry, but the new family can still provide some of its basic functions, such as shelter, food, and loving care. While many people claim that divorce is destroying the family, some experts remind us that divorce is not a rejection of the family but of a spouse. The family, although smaller or larger, remains.

Adjusting to a changing family can be very difficult. Sometimes it is comforting just to know that other people have lived through situations that are similar or worse than yours or your friends'. Most of all, it is good to know that tomorrow can be brighter.

2

COMING UNGLUED

"The only thing worse than divorce is death," Grammy remarked the day after Mike's parents told him they were going to separate. On that day, Mike, who was an only child, agreed with her.

Mike's family had been sitting around the kitchen table the night before. His parents had seemed preoccupied during supper, and after the dishes had been cleared away, his father announced that he was leaving that night. He and Mike's mother were going to live in different houses from now on. Mike's father said that he and Mom had not been getting along well for some time. Mike knew this to be true, for his parents constantly quarreled. Mike had grown to take this for granted.

Mike held himself very still. Even the kitchen seemed strangely quiet as his father explained that everyone argues from time to time, but he and Mom disagreed almost every time they spoke to each other. They irritated each other so much that they both decided it was time to separate. It was time for a divorce.

Mike felt like crying, but he held back the tears. He didn't say anything at all because there were too many things that he wanted to ask all at once. He had questions about what was going to happen to him. Where would he live? What had he done to cause the separation?

Mike squirmed in his chair while his mother spoke to him about the problems she and Dad were having. She explained that they had made many mistakes during their marriage and now their mistakes were beyond repair. She said that she was sorry she had been cross to Mike at times when she felt unhappy. Some of the times she had been cross with Mike she had really been upset with Dad.

While his mother and father continued to talk to him, Mike wondered about what he would tell his friends. What would they say? Some of them had parents who no longer lived together. Some of them seemed to manage living with mothers part of the time and with fathers part of the time. Mike had always thought this could never happen in his family.

Finally, Mike asked, "What will happen to me?"

"You will live with me, Mike," his mother told him. "I've seen a smaller house I like. It will be more convenient for both of us. As soon as we get things cleared up here, we'll move there. Your Dad is taking a job in another city. It's about a thousand miles away from here."

"I'll still love you, Mike," his father assured him. "I will always love you and help to take care of you."

Mike wondered how his father could take care of him when he was so far away, but he didn't say anything. He was more concerned now about where he and his mother would live. He felt somewhat better when he learned that the new house would be in the same school district. Joe, one of the boys in his class, had moved from another part of the country because his parents had separated. Joe still seemed very lost. Mike thought he would make a special effort to be nice to him when he saw him tomorrow.

Mike asked to be excused. He left the table quietly and went to watch television. The television set was in the next room and even when Mike turned it on, he could hear his parents telling each other that things went well and that he did not seem very upset. Somehow he couldn't show them how awful he felt. He loved both his mother and his father and wanted to be with them both. He yearned to ask them to reconsider and he tried to think of how he could persuade them to get together again, but he felt frozen inside himself.

As the days went by, and Mike thought more and more about the divorce plans, he grew certain that he was responsible. Mike had heard his father say several times that he could not live in the house any longer, and Mike remembered things that he had done each time that had upset his father. For example, he remembered his father saying this the day after Mike had broken the glass top of the coffee table. Another time his father stayed out all night after Mike had spilled a box of cereal all over the kitchen floor. Mike did not realize that his father had barely noticed these things. He had no way of knowing that his father was too busy with his own problems.

It was many weeks before Mike's feelings improved so that he disagreed with Grammy's statement that the only thing worse than divorce is death. He had a new friend in Joe, who listened to his problems and pointed out that there were even some new things that were good. The house was very peaceful without his parents' constant quarreling.

FEELING GUILTY

Many young people feel that they are the cause of their parents' divorce, as Mike did. This is especially true around the time of separation. They associate their own behavior with their parents' problems even though the children may have had nothing at all to do with them.

Many children express their feeling of guilt in the following ways: "My allowance was too big. If I don't take any allowance for the next year, you will not have to fight over money." "I'll stop quarreling with my sister, then you will be happier and Dad will not have to leave." "I promise not to be bad anymore."

Why do so many young people think they are guilty? Psychiatrists believe that the child's feeling guilty about the separation involves a notion of control even though this notion is not realized. A child feels helpless about changing his parents' minds to go ahead with a divorce, but if the child was the cause of their decision to separate, he or she could do something to bring about a reversal of the decision.

For example, Kim felt very guilty about the trouble she had caused by staying out beyond the time her parents set for her to come home. She had caused many arguments about this, she knew, and she had even convinced her mother that her father was being overly strict. When Kim learned of her parents' plans for divorce, she promised to obey her father's rules for being home on time. She even offered to come home earlier than the time he set.

Kim was so distressed she discussed her guilty feelings with her counselor at school, even though she did not enjoy talking about her family with strangers. The counselor explained to her that there were some things that she could change and some things over which she had no control. He told Kim that her hopes of preventing her parents from separating with better behavior were not realistic. He stressed that Kim must resign herself to the reality that she was not the cause of the problem. What Kim had done in the past had not caused the divorce plans, and what she did in the future would not change them. The counselor helped Kim to recognize that there were some things that she could do to help lessen the pain of separation. When Kim recognized this, she stopped feeling guilty.

Many counselors and therapists help young people who feel responsible for their parents' separation by explaining the unconscious desire for control. They help young people to see the dynamics of divorce, looking at it through the eyes of parents rather than through their own eyes. They point out that children are not usually the cause of problems in a husband-wife relationship, and help the boys and girls understand that parents divorce each other, not their children. When children recognize that it is not within their power to control certain things, such as divorce, the feeling of being responsible is lifted. Then they can proceed to doing the things that they *can* control, such as developing positive things in their lives. For example, they can involve themselves in more meaningful relationships with other children and adults to try to make up for the partial or total absence of a parent.

Even though parents reassure a child that the decision to divorce rests entirely on their own problems and that the child is in no way at fault, they are not usually believed. In a group of thirty junior high school students of divorced parents who met weekly, twenty-eight expressed the belief that they were to blame for their parents' divorce. At first, many blamed one parent, then the other, but eventually they blamed themselves. In most cases, the blaming was silent and would not have been expressed except for the group discussion in which the counselor asked a direct question about blame. Privately, they had been telling themselves time after time, "I'm hopeless." "If I had been better, Mom would not have started to drown her troubles in drink." "I can't do anything right." "I'd better stop making mistakes, or I'll cause trouble for other people the way I did for my mother and father."

Unfortunately, by silently accepting the blame for a divorce one can interfere with one's feelings throughout a lifetime. This blame can lower self-esteem, a quality on which much growth depends. A child's actions may play a major part in causing a divorce, but this is seldom the case. Most of the children who feel guilty see their part as greater than it really is.

FEELING LOST

Many kinds of feelings can get mixed up when family members separate. One very common feeling among children of divorced parents is that of abandonment. One very young child lived with his father after his mother left the family. They walked in the park together every afternoon.

Whenever the child saw a woman who looked slightly like his mother coming toward him, he would run ahead of his father and throw himself at the woman. He would cling to her until he could be convinced that she was not his mother. One time after he accepted that the woman he was hugging was not really his mother, the boy cried openly. Then he clung to his father and begged his father not to leave him.

Feeling abandoned and concerned that the remaining parent will leave is a common experience for many children of divorce. Consider the case of seven-year-old Martha, whose mother and father often told her how awful the other one was. Martha's father complained he was ignored by his family. No one was interested in his work or his guitar playing—a hobby that absorbed most of his time. Her mother felt neglected, too, and claimed that the father had no time for his family. After they separated, Martha's mother announced that her father had deserted them for the woman who lived down the street. Actually, the father did leave quietly one night without saying goodbye to Martha or giving her any assurance that he would ever see her again.

Martha slept poorly after her father left home. She called her mother often during the night and said she heard noises that might be her father coming back to his room. Although the mother explained that he would not come home again to live with them, she tried to comfort the little girl and told Martha that she might be able to visit him in his new home. But the restless nights continued. And some nights Martha thought she heard her mother packing her bags. She feared that she might slip away as her father had. Martha's fears developed into nightmares of being abandoned and stopped only when she saw a therapist who helped her to understand and believe that her mother would not abandon her, too.

Then there is Eric. Eric tried very hard to be good. He had been told that his mother had sent his "bad" father away, and he did not want this to happen to him. His good behavior made his mother very happy until she began to realize that something was wrong. Eric seemed always on guard and too eager to please. His mother began to wonder if Eric really meant what he said or if he was telling her what he thought she wanted to hear. Actually, this made Eric's mother angry with him because he was not being frank with her. By trying to be good he was not himself, and this made him uncomfortable. Eric and his mother discussed the problem, and Eric felt better when his mother assured him that she would not send him away, no matter what he did.

Even when a parent can't visit a child because he or she lives too far away, some children of divorced parents interpret the loss as abandonment. There are cases where boys and girls are so afraid of being abandoned by the remaining parent that they use a variety of maneuvers to deny the fear. For example, they play with matches, they heedlessly run across streets in front of traffic, and they climb in dangerous places. Psychiatrists sometimes attribute these actions to children's attempts to prove that they cannot be harmed. This kind of behavior is sometimes a bid for attention, which is meant to make the parent stay close by to watch and protect the child. Many children are helped only with the knowledge that the parent who left the family has abandoned his or her spouse, not the child.

Some children see their parents' behavior at the time of a family's breaking apart as childish, and lose their sense of trust in them. The children feel unprotected because their parents seem unable to care even for themselves. Sometimes remarks made by one parent about the other parent's worthlessness cause the child to feel concerned or lost. But as time goes on children grow to realize that this was a time of crisis when many remarks were exaggerated. There is comfort for some in knowing that even if both parents were to abandon them, a situation that is unlikely to happen, grandparents or other adults would care for them.

Parents who do not have custody of their children express their interest in different degrees. They vary on one extreme from those who consider the child first in their lives to those who break completely with their offspring. Both of these extremes may be harmful, depending on the particular situation, but the parent who completely ignores a child may be the most difficult for a child to understand. Sometimes, the remaining parent makes excuses for the neglectful one, to protect the children from feelings of abandonment. The mother may make remarks such as "Your father really loves you. He just does not know how to show his love." Or when a birthday is forgotten, the father may say, "Your mother never did have a very good memory." Young children see their parents as infallible, and therefore it is traumatic for them to realize that a parent has failed in any way, and to recognize that both parents cannot be right.

Fortunately, there are very few parents who cut themselves off completely from their children. In some cases, the problem is complicated. Some may try to make a complete break with the other parent in spite of the harm to the child. The custodial parent may try to make a complete break with the other parent, thinking that this may be the best for the children. Some may cut off contact with the other parent for selfish reasons, ignoring their children's needs.

In Paul's case, it was the mother who was selfish. Ten-year-old Paul was the oldest of three children. He had responded to his father's departure by curling up in a closet and sobbing for long periods of time. Now and then, he would telephone his father and beg him to return. Paul was very frightened about the future and he felt torn into two pieces. As time passed, Paul sided entirely with his mother, who continued to attack the father verbally. For example, the mother told the children that they would have to give up their dog because their father was not providing enough money for dog food. Actually, he was supplying a large amount of support money, but they had no way of knowing that their father had not abandoned them.

Several months after Paul's initial response to the separation in which he hid in the closet, Paul stopped pleading with his father to return. He helped his mother to turn his sisters against the father and rejected his father's attempts to see the family. He even returned his gifts.

All the children in this family felt abandoned by the father even though he really was trying desperately to have a good relationship with them. The mother was working out her anger at her ex-husband by using the children. In some cases, such as this, a parent just gives up trying to see the children, even though the desire is there. The deceit of one parent hurts and confuses the rest of the family.

Many therapists feel that there is something seriously wrong with a person who does not express love for a child. Mary was an unusually mature girl who was able to understand this. She could appreciate the fact that just because her father did not show love for her did not mean that she was unlovable. Friends and other adults love her now and many will do so in the future. The defect is with her parent, not with her. Unfortunately, this is very difficult, if not impossible, for most children to understand. Children in this situation may well be angry at the neglectful parent. Many feel depressed. It is more appropriate to have a feeling of pity for the person who is missing the rich experience of loving and rearing one's own child, but a child would find this very difficult to believe under these circumstances.

Some degree of rejection by a parent is not the same as total abandonment. A parent who wishes to be with a child may find times when seeing the child is very inconvenient, or actually impossible. This does not mean that the parent does not love the child. In all human relationships, there are complications and mood swings. Just because a parent grows angry with a child, or is bored with a relationship from time to time, or even several times in one day, does not mean that the parent does not love the child. Many parents have problems that take a great deal of their time and make them irritable or prevent the free expression of love. They do not explain this to their children, and therefore the children draw the wrong conclusion from their actions. They think their parents do not love them.

There are only a small percentage of fathers and mothers who really do not love their children. These adults have many good qualities but are deficient in their ability to love. Such parents do not enjoy doing things with their children. They do not want to hold them or touch them, even for a second or two. They do not show pride in their children or in their children's accomplishments, and they really do not want to spend time with them. If you think a parent does not love you, it may only seem that way. You may need to talk this over with an adult counselor who is trained to look at the situation from many sides.

Some boys and girls try many ways to get a parent to show interest in them. For example, acting naughty or too good are ways of gaining attention. Many children find it difficult to accept the fact that a parent is not perfect, and some refuse to do so. They make idols of the absent parent, using all kinds of excuses for the neglect. Many of these children find gratification if they are helped by Scout leaders, Big Brothers or Big Sisters, and leaders in some of the organizations mentioned on pages 105-109.

FEELING SAD

Divorce makes most children sad at first. Many go through a period of mourning that is not as intense as that when a parent dies but it follows the same stages. At first, they find it impossible to believe that their family has come unglued. Then they become sad because they do not see one parent as often as before and memories of the missing person fill the mind. Crying is a good way to express this sadness. Angry feelings and guilty feelings follow, although many of these stages overlap. This grief is a process by which one reaches a stage of healthy detachment from the past and makes it possible to reach out for new experiences. Even though the sadness at the loss of the original family may never leave completely, it need not keep one from having a happy and full life.

Jim felt very depressed for several weeks after his father left. Then he began to feel better after he became involved with helping to set up the new living arrangements. Even though he grumbled about doing some of the household chores, it made him feel better to be responsible for the same unpleasant everyday tasks that he had always done. Certainly, much in his life had changed. Like almost all children who experience the divorce of parents, he wished that the family would reunite. Jim wanted his father to come back, and he wished all aspects of his life would return to normal. Even though his mother and father had argued much of the time, he wanted the days to be the way they used to be. He found there was a certain amount of comfort for him in the familiar. But like most human beings, Jim was resilient. After a few weeks, he accepted his sadness at the loss of his father's day-to-day presence and began to make a new life for himself.

In certain cases, the time after divorce can be better in some ways than the time when parents were arguing, or when an alcoholic parent caused problems for the family, or when some other very difficult situation existed. Although children are sad and they miss the absent parent, there is a sense of relief in having a more peaceful home.

Even the young people who find life terribly sad immediately after parents separate discover that they can get used to living in a single-parent household or a new situation. The painful feelings hurt less and less. There are even cases where boys and girls see more of their fathers after a divorce than they did when the family was supposedly intact. In any case, feelings of sadness and helplessness seldom last very long.

FEELING ANGRY

Boys and girls of all ages are angry about the divorce of their parents and, to some degree, feelings of anger at such a time are reasonable. Adolescents may be especially angry because they feel that their parents' separation has increased their problems at an especially difficult time in their lives. Some condemn both parents for the way they have acted, while others are angry with just one parent. Imagine how you would feel if you could no longer respect the parent you have especially admired and identified with. You would feel angry and disappointed because you could no longer look to that parent as a guide.

Recognizing the anger that comes at separation is often difficult, but expressing anger, talking about it, and exploring the reasons for it helps to resolve these feelings. Denying that anger can make things worse. Repressing the anger may mean that it is channeled into a neurotic behavior. One boy became very conscious of his nose after his father left home. Not only did he spend a great deal of time thinking about his nose and looking at it in the mirror, but he noticed other people's noses and compared them with his own. He had no idea that this obsession with noses was at all related to his feelings of guilt and hostility at losing his father until a doctor helped him work out his problems.

When the causes of anger are not recognized, the hostility felt after a parents' divorce can be expressed in an unlimited number of ways. For example, a boy may equate antisocial behavior with masculinity, a view encouraged by many television programs. Since he is living with a female parent, he may fear that some of her femininity may rub off on him and make him unmanly. He may also identify with the absent male parent through attempts to prove his masculinity. He chooses friends who belong to a tough gang that considers shoplifting, vandalism, and other anti-social behavior a mark of masculinity, unaware that this is his way of expressing his anger, and gaining a false sense of power.

Mark, on the other hand, was a boy who had already expressed his anger directly so there was no need for acting angry when he was asked to join a gang of boys that were heavily involved in the drug scene. He considered joining them, but he felt secure in spite of the fact that his parents were divorced. He knew that they both loved him, even though they no longer loved each other. When one of the boys called him "chicken" for not trying a capsule of unknown contents, Mark was comfortable about refusing. He chided them about taking the capsule. He said it was a stupid thing to do, not something brave or daring.

Some children engage in destructive acts to try to gain the attention of a parent, such as running in traffic, excessive dieting, or engaging in other hazardous activities. They may unconsciously feel that punishment is better than no attention at all, but later they find that this further alienates the parent for whom they are reaching. Acting out, or undesirable behavior may also be an expression of depression by children who suffer from sadness rather than anger.

INSTANT ADULT

Sue was an only child who was expected to act like an adult. Both her mother and father were very ambitious about getting ahead. They expected Sue to excel in everything she did. Sue's father had traveled a great deal for many years and her mother had spent each and every day doing volunteer work at the local hospital. Sue's mother grew more and more involved with the hospital programs and she was delighted when she was invited to join the trustees, most of whom were men. There were many night meetings, so Sue had to take over many of the family chores that would normally have been done by her mother. She was able to manage this well until her father stopped traveling and she was put in the role of home-maker for her father. Sue was upset by this, but her mother would not give up her volunteer activi-ties. When Sue's mother became interested in one of the doctors at the hospital and moved out of the house, both her parents agreed to a divorce. Sue was left at home to care for her father. He seemed jealous of her friends and talked with her much as he would talk to someone his own age. Sue felt the heavy burden of his problems. She thought about running away, but she found help from the coun-selor at school, who persuaded her father to talk over his problems with a psychiatrist or psycholo-gist.

Many parents use their children as a substitute for a missing spouse. Ralph was glad that his mother did not expect him to be "the man of the house" after her divorce. She made it clear that he was not expected to "make up for Daddy now that he is away." She would still make the big deci-sions, although she promised to discuss some things with him. Ralph was glad he did not have to listen to the people who told him, "Now that your father is gone, you will have to take care of your mother."

TODAY IS NOT FOREVER

Feelings of sadness, hurt, anger, and anxiety are common at the time a family is coming unglued. Although people handle these feelings in different ways, it is good to know that it is healthy to express some of these emotions by discussing them. Children and parents are distressed by divorce, but the distress lessens with time. Bit by bit, most children and parents find that they have not lost their happy selves forever. Just knowing this can help.

3

LIVING WITH ONE PARENT

The Father-Son Dinner notices were fun for everyone in the class but Tim. His father lived far away and he never saw him unless there was a holiday, when Tim was shipped off for a visit. Tim's teacher suggested that he bring an uncle or a friend of the family to the dinner. Tim had done this last year shortly after his parents were divorced and he had a good time, but it was not the same. He really missed his father. Now that the intense pain and suffering of the period immediately following the separation had disappeared, Tim had a sad, resigned attitude about the divorce. Most of the time he did not think much about the loss of his father in everyday family life. It was just on occasions like the Father-Son Dinner when the whole bad scene came back to him.

Tim was not the only one in his class who did not live with his father. One of the girls never knew her father; her mother had never married. Another boy saw his father on weekends and lived with his mother during the week. Since this boy's father lived nearby, he would come to the dinner. One boy had a stepfather who had been around ever since he could remember. He had no problem about asking him to the Father-Son Dinner.

As many as one boy and girl in five lives with just one parent. In 1980, it was reported that about 45 percent of the children born in any one year were expected to live with only one of their parents at some time before they reached the age of eighteen. In that same year, 20 percent of the elementary school children and 15 percent of secondary school children in a survey of eighteen thousand children lived in single-parent houses. While single-parent families are more common in some parts of the United States than in others, this study was spread out in fourteen states throughout the country.

Some children find living with a single parent very difficult, while others get along as well or even better than some of the children who live with two parents. This is especially true when the parents do not get along well.

SINGLE-PARENT HOMES CAN BE SECURE

There are many studies about the impact of divorce on children. Most show that the separation of parents is an acutely painful experience for children. Still, they indicate that one stable and well-functioning parent within a home can make a child feel secure and grow normally. When problems between a parent and child persist, it is quite possible that some of the trouble may have been there before the divorce or might have developed anyway. Some authorities even see divorce as a challenge. With enough support from parents, children learn to develop their own resources and gain a sense of mastery while doing so.

Consider the problem of twelve-year-old Jean, who was so overprotected that she was never allowed to make decisions. Everytime her friends asked her to go to the corner store with them, Jean had to ask her mother. Her mother decided what clothes she should wear each day, she planned her activities, chose her playmates, and did most of Jean's thinking for her. Jean was more protected than ever after her parents separated. Her mother had no interests in life other than Jean, and she really felt that she was being a good mother by devoting all of her time to her daughter. Unfortunately, when Jean became an adolescent, she rebelled against all authority and ran away from home. She was exposed to young people who introduced her to drugs and prostitution. Both she and her mother encountered crisis situations for which they were ill-prepared.

Rachel, on the other hand, grew up in a family where she was encouraged to make her own decisions. Although her parents were strict about setting limits they encouraged Rachel to solve problems by using her own resources whenever the opportunity arose. Rachel was better able to deal with the emotional problems that all children of divorce encounter to some degree after her parents separated. She was encouraged to continue to be competent. Her self-confidence helped her to meet the crisis of losing contact with her father and to make a good home life with her mother that was free of the constant arguing that had been part of her life before.

Each person's situation differs a great deal and the cases mentioned above are two extremes. Each parent and each child is unique, but there are some patterns that can be recognized and changed before serious problems develop. For example, if the anger, sadness, feelings of abandonment, and other early reactions to separation have not begun to fade by the end of a year and a young person living with a single parent is still miserable, the help of a counselor may be needed.

LIFE FOR MOTHER

Many young people who live with one parent are aware of the special problems that a mother or father alone may have. Divorce is a very painful experience for parents too. Many times, a single parent combines the long hours of earning a living with the day-to-day problems of parenting. When single-parent families have been part of a two-parent family at some time but have lost one parent because of death or divorce, the social life of the single parent in a family is different from that of the role played in a family where there are two parents. Many single parents suffer from fear, loneliness, isolation, guilt, failure, and other negative emotions. Their children bury their fears and become more insecure.

Just as children must make many adjustments after separation, parents have to learn to live in a different kind of world. For some it is better, for some it is worse. For all, it is a time of change.

Mrs. Singer was very lonely after her divorce. She thought most of her friends sided with her husband. Actually they decided to ignore the Singers so they would not be accused of taking sides. Mrs. Singer tried to make new friends so that she would not have to depend entirely on the children for companionship. First, she joined a woman's club, but she found that most of the members were cool to her. Even though she volunteered to help with some of the activities, she did not feel that she was part of the group whose families were still intact. Besides, the schedule conflicted with her part-time job as a waitress. Since she had never worked outside the home before, she found the job especially exhausting.

However, Mrs. Singer continued to reach out to other adults. She thought she might make new friends by taking an evening course at the local high school. She did discover that the people in her class were friendly before and after class, but no one really seemed interested in spending any time with her outside of the classroom. The next semester, she took a course that offered field trips to study the historic buildings in the area. Here she had a better chance to chat with people. One member of the class was a woman whose husband had just left her, and she was glad to meet someone like Mrs. Singer who would join new groups with her. As her life grew more interesting, Mrs. Singer became more relaxed at home and she was able to deal with her children's problems more easily. She even found it helpful to discuss her decisions about them with several members of a group that ran a thrift shop for the hospital. This helped her to set limits and enforce rules that made family life run more smoothly.

In the single-parent family, there is only one parent who is responsible for rules and this can seem overwhelming to the parent. For a child, it may make life simpler. Certainly, Ellen's life was more comfortable. Before her parents were divorced, Ellen's mother kept one set of rules and her father insisted on another. Ellen knew she could start an argument any time she wanted to by telling her father that she did not have to be home at the time he set because her mother said this time was unreasonable. Now that there was one less opinion to be reckoned with, there was more stability in the home.

Many single parents feel overwhelmed with the responsibilities that come with tending to children's needs, earning money, paying bills, and handling all the everyday matters that were once shared by two people. Some discover that they have little time for themselves and this makes them depressed. Since depression drains energy from an individual, the situation grows worse.

Children who are old enough to understand that a parent needs some time and energy for personal pleasures can help by taking some of the responsibility for running the house. They may discover that this participation helps make life better for them, too.

THE GOOD WITH THE BAD

According to some experts, the children in a single-parent home may have an advantage because their help is needed in doing household chores. In a two-parent house, there may be nothing left for a child to do other than watch television or play. There is no participation with other members of the family in washing cars, doing housework, cooking meals, and other chores of that nature. Understanding this point of view may be very difficult for the people doing the chores, but there is real value in working with other members of the family.

Another interesting advantage has been observed for some college students who come from single-parent homes. A number of studies suggest that children who share in the home management with their mothers in single-parent homes exhibit greater verbal skills than children in two-parent homes. Perhaps this is due to their closeness to the mother. For example, a study of men who were entering Stanford University showed that students who lived in single-parent homes with their mothers for at least one year in their childhood scored higher than other students in the language part of aptitude tests. The scores were no lower in mathmatical sections. This may or may not be true for those who spent time in a single-parent home in which the father was the only parent.

Many experts are finding that divorce may offer some benefits for both parents and children after the initial difficult times pass. Like two-parent homes, single-parent homes may be places that are happy or unhappy. Although there may be many periods of confusion and conflict, it is possible to come though the experience with few scars and to turn the challenges into periods of growth.

LIFE FOR FATHER

While most of the children who live with a single parent live with a mother, more and more are spending most of their time with a father. Nine out of ten children of divorce in the past were assigned to the care of their mothers with or without visitation rights for the father. The father was considered as the one to care for the children most of the time only if the mother was considered unfit for moral reasons or on account of some emotional or physical handicap. Today, some mothers are choosing careers in which the full-time care of children intereferes and they are relieved to have the children reside with the father. And many fathers seem glad to take advantage of the trend for men to exhibit more nurturing qualities. They feel quite capable and successful in their ability to be the primary parent for their children, even though not all of these fathers grew up in families where they learned to mend, clean house, and do many of the other household chores. Along with working mothers, single fathers enlist the help of their older children and lean on groups such as Big Sisters, Big Brothers, and Foster Grandparents for support. Their pride in being able to cope with the challenge of parenthood and watching their children mature under their guidance usually makes up for the problems caused by their inexperience in running a house and the many adjustments they must make.

TWO PARENTS IN ONE?

Some parents tend to overcompensate for the absent parent by trying to be both mother and father to their children. There is more concern about boys than girls. Some believe a fatherless boy may be less aggressive or more effeminate than one raised by both parents, and that later in life he may have difficulty in his role as a husband and father. Even though a parent of the same sex serves as a role model for the child's own sex role, however, there has been no evidence to suggest that it is necessary to have a father in the home in order for boys to learn the nature of the roles, responsibilities, and behaviors considered appropriate to men. Just as children whose parents speak no English can soon learn to speak the language fluently from people outside the home, older brothers, older boys in the neighborhood, Big Brothers, uncles, and neighbors can serve as role models for the traditional masculine traits. It may be comforting for the boys in a fatherless home to know that the images on television that show boys and their fathers spending a lot of time fishing, building models, and playing touch football do not always reflect real life for most boys.

According to Dr. James Turnbill of the University of Texas Health Science Center, fathers in middle- and lower-income families spend only about twenty-five minutes each week in direct one-to-one contact with their sons. The mother's attitude toward men and the degree to which she allows the boy freedom to develop his own identity seem to be the key to his development in a fatherless home. This whole subject of the importance of masculine traits versus feminine traits is one of controversy in today's world, but many psychiatrists, psychologists, and other experts still feel that it is important for boys and girls to have a role model of the same sex.

Some experts believe that girls living with their mothers as head of the household show a special craving for male attention, but it has been shown that boys who live in fatherless families also crave male attention. This may be due to a need for all young children of divorce to regain a father figure. One might expect to find a special craving for women when children live with a father as the only parent.

The presence of role models does appear to help children with sex identification as do positive comments about people of a child's own sex from the parent of the opposite sex. The most important years for sex identification come between the ages of thirty months and five years, and at early adolescence. Perhaps you can help by acting as a role model for a sister or for a young person in your neighborhood who lives in a single-parent family.

PARENTS WITHOUT PARTNERS

No matter whether a single parent is a mother or a father, the most important source of security for boys and girls is a competent, self-confident parent. Many single-parent families find practical solutions to some of their problems through organizations such as Parents Without Partners. This organization began on a hot summer day at a beach back in 1956 when two divorced people were discussing how different their lives had become from what they had been and from the lives of their married friends. They wondered if getting together with other single parents might be a helpful learning experience for everyone involved in the situation. The next spring, these people placed some ads in newspapers inviting any parents without partners to a meeting where they could talk over common problems, develop a fuller life for themselves and their children, and hold discussions with psychologists and lawyers. The first meeting was held in a room provided by a church in New York City. The organization grew from this small beginning to become an international one with about 188,000 members and 1,100 chapters in less than 25 years. There are members in all fifty states and most of the Canadian provinces. People in many countries have used the Parents Without Partners as a model to form similar groups. About 85 percent of the members of Parents Without Partners are single through separation or divorce, and the rest are either widowed, natural parents who never married, or single adoptive parents.

Many adults join local chapters of Parents Without Partners because their children urge them to do so. Many young people learn about the family activities they offer from other boys and girls in the classes. For example, one is a car clinic run by fathers who are mechanics and interested in young people. Chapters may have community service programs, puppetry, creative-writing classes, softball games, and other sports, and/or any of about two hundred different activities. All chapters have some programs. In addition to meeting people who live in single-parent families in these family activities, parents and children share in many valuable experiences through them.

Beside the family activities and the sharing of ideas between parents at adult meetings, some areas have formed chapters known as The International Youth Council. These chapters are open to adolescents between the ages of twelve and seventeen whose parents are separated, divorced, widowed, or never married. Although many of the parents are members of Parents Without Partners, this is not necessary for a young person to join. Advisors help with educational, recreational, and community-service programs. Panel discussions may include getting along with parents, discipline problems, disc jockeys, allowances, drugs, part-time jobs, and numerous other subjects. One International Youth Council chapter planned an outing they called "Night Owl Bus Ride" on which they visited police stations, hospitals, and night court. Then they had breakfast at dawn at a favorite eating place. Another chapter raised funds so that they could take a week's canoe trip. Another provided a program of entertainment and games for a children's institution. Many such programs help the members to develop independence, responsibility, and leadership.

SINGLE-PARENT FAMILY CENTERS

Many small organizations have sprung up throughout the United States to answer various needs of single-parent families. For example, at some Young Men's & Young Women's Christian Associations (YM-YWCA'S) and at some Young Men's & Young Women's Hebrew Associations (YM-YWHA's) there are special groups for parents and for children that help them explore their feelings about divorce and the problems of living in a single-parent family. There are some groups that have clothing swaps, food co-ops, baby-sitting pools, joint vacations, and pot-luck suppers. The latter are especially welcomed by many families who find that the dinner hour is difficult because the absent parent is missed specially at the table. The traditional family meal that was formerly a happy time is often a lonely time. Late evening is another difficult period when many single parents find comfort on hotlines that are run by single-parent volunteers. Advice on how to get a job, find a lawyer, obtain welfare benefits and housing, or just the sound of another adult voice helps the callers. Many community-service organizations and neighborhood associations organize hotlines for single parents and for people with a variety of problems.

Schools are becoming more aware of the needs of children who live in one-parent families. In some cases, the school tries to fill some of the empty space left by the absent parent, but this is unusual. Few school budgets allow for this kind of parent-teacher interaction. Many single parents who have young children find that day-care centers provide the warmth of a missing parent until they finish work. They know that a child who needs loving can't be asked to wait until mother comes home at 6 P.M. But time is needed to compensate. Many mothers involved in tight schedules see that there is a time devoted entirely to their children. For example, one mother scheduled two hours every evening for her three-year-old daughter and let nothing interfere with that time. The hours between 6 and 8 P.M. belonged to the two of them and they were very special hours for both.

FROM "BROKEN HOMES" TO FAMILY UNITS

Being a child or teenager in a single-parent home might have seemed unusual ten years ago.

The stigma that went with the old name "broken home" is disappearing. Classmates are often in similar situations today and it is more common to find teachers who understand the unique and special needs of single-parent families from their own personal experiences. Today, it is realized that, with special effort, a single-parent home can provide the same security, warmth, and psychological nourishment for the healthy development of children as a two-parent home can.

CUSTODY AND PARENTAL KIDNAPPING

"What will happen to me?" is one of the first questions children ask when hearing of their parents' plan to separate. Many parents determine where their children will live before they tell them about the divorce plans so they can readily answer the question. For some families, however, custody is a serious and continuing problem.

When ten-year-old Bobby was asked to draw a picture of how he felt about his family after a two-year custody battle, he drew a boy hanging on a tightrope that was stretched over a deep valley. A parent stood on either side at the top of a mountain holding the ends of the rope. When asked what his parents were saying, Bobby told the counselor that both mother and father were trying to bribe his allegiance with promises of things he wanted. Bobby was hanging rather precariously in the picture; it seemed to express the fear that he might fall into the valley and be destroyed.

47

Another child who was asked to draw a picture of her family at the time of a custody battle drew her mother and her brother with her but did not show her father. When asked what the father looked like, she replied, "A greedy ape."

Fortunately, most custody agreements are worked out for "the best interests of the child" without long years of legal hassles, but not everyone agrees about what is best. Certainly, the best arrangment for one family may not be the best for another family.

TYPES OF LIVING ARRANGEMENTS

In the most common type of custody, children live with one parent and spend some time with the other one. The arrangement is specified in the divorce decree. Until the early part of this century, children were generally assigned to the care of the father since he was considered the head of the household. As ideas about the role of women in child rearing grew in importance, the courts presumed that the best interests of the child were served by placing him or her with the mother.

Although mothers now get sole custody in the great majority of cases, there is a trend toward joint custody. This arrangement, which is known as shared custody or divided custody, is one in which parents share equal responsibility in caring for the children. Those who believe in joint custody claim that prejudice in favor of mothers is based on outdated sex roles. Many fathers are not as poor at nurturing as they were once thought to be. In fact, many fathers are as good or better than their ex-wives. One reason for favoring mothers in placing children with one parent in the past was the fact that most of the women stayed at home. This is no longer true; more than half the number of divorced women now work outside the home.

In some areas of the United States fathers have joined together in groups such as Equal Rights for Fathers and Fathers for Equal Justice to work toward bringing about changes in the routine assignment of children to the mothers. A number of states now have laws authorizing joint custody and even require judges to start with the presumption of joint custody.

Joint custody is growing in popularity. For example, it is estimated that 20 percent of the children of divorced parents in Los Angeles, California, shuttle between their parents' homes on a variety of time schedules.

Whether or not you consider the trend toward joint custody a good one depends somewhat on which expert you follow. Some authorities, such as Dr. Richard A. Gardner, Dr. Lee Salk, and Dr. Benjamin Spock, agree that joint custody can be a positive experience for children if parents can deal comfortably with the decision-making that is involved. Dr. Melvin Roman, a professor of psychiatry at Albert Einstein College of Medicine of Yeshiva University, believes that joint custody is the preferred arrangement for most children and that half of the parents separated by divorce could succeed at it with proper counseling. Another highly respected psychiatrist, Dr. Albert J. Solnit, director of Yale University's Child Study Center, feels that it is important for a child to know that one adult will have responsibility for his or her daily care. He suggests that joint custody is something like two half-anchors for a child who needs an anchor. There is much controversy about benefits of such arrangements for the child. Some experts insist that one caretaker is better; however, it is predicted that sharing children will be the most common custody arrangement by 1990.

Split custody is different from joint custody although it amounts to sole custody as far as children are concerned. In this arrangement siblings are separated so that different parents have full responsibility. Usually the boys live with the father and the girls with the mother, but this is not always the way they are divided. As with other arrangements, the individual situation has to be considered. Some psychiatrists feel that, in general, split custody is not a good arrangement. There may be a double trauma: having to cope with the divorce and the possible loss of siblings. Brothers and sisters can be very supportive of each other in times of crisis or when parents are absent. In all cases, parents and judges are supposed to work toward the best interests of the child even if the child does not think, at the time, that the arrangement is the best one.

There is general agreement that children under the age of twelve should be consulted about custody, but that the final decision about what is best should be left to adults. Young children are not mature enough to know which parent can and is willing to make the best home for them. Besides, asking a child to choose one parent over another may provoke anxiety and guilt about loyalty. It is a no-win situation. The requests of adolescents are usually considered more seriously than those of young children. Even then, choices may be made for superficial reasons such as the promise of a private telephone.

The best arrangements are flexible enough to change as people change. This works best when parents remain friendly.

VISITS WITH FATHER

Mary's home life was patterned to fit the orders of a divorce decree that gave her mother sole custody. Every other weekend and one night a week was to be spent with her father. This was not always convenient for Mary or for her parents, but they tried to follow the arrangement as much as possible. Sometimes, Mary traded weekends at the request of her father. Sometimes she changed the schedule because of her own plans. She especially dreaded Wednesday nights when she would have to take the bus to her father's apartment on the far side of town. Then she would have to get up early the next morning so that she could make the long ride back to school in time for her first class. Mary really enjoyed seeing her father, but she wished her parents still lived in the same house.

When Mary's father had to go away for six months she felt rather guilty about feeling glad.

This meant she would be able to forget about the weekend visits and the inconvenience of Wednesday night. Two weeks after her father had left, however, Mary wished he would come home again so she could talk to him. He had always understood how difficult it was for Mary to visit him and he was always ready to spend time listening to her other problems. Long before the six months were up, Mary found that she was looking forward to getting back to the old schedule.

"DISNEYLAND DAD"

Melissa spent one weekend a month with her father, a man who confused love with presents. Each time he came for her he had a new surprise. It seemed that the whole weekend was spent in going to the zoo or the amusement park, the movies, or some other place that her father thought she would like. The visits were full of excitement, but there was a great deal of tension, and this made Melissa feel uncomfortable. Going places some of the time was good, but she would have preferred spending some time with her father, fixing her bicycle with him, or just shopping together for a new pair of sneakers. She wished they could have entertained each other by just talking to each other rather than always being entertained by someone or something else. Sometimes it almost seemed that her father was trying to buy her affection.

Actually, Melissa's father was exhausted after each visit. He would have welcomed a quiet day with her in which they could have exchanged opinions, talked about interests they shared, and acted more naturally. Melissa hoped that someday she would have the courage to ask her father if they could just spend some quiet days together even if she had to take the chance of hurting his feelings.

Making an appointment to be with a parent can be very artificial, and it is easy to understand why some parents wonder how they can best spend the short time that they have with their children. Visitation is a time for the parent and children to be with each other and enjoy each other. Although it is sometimes helpful to include a friend on a visit with a "weekend parent," time alone for discussing things can help to keep a positive relationship. Giving a father or mother a chance to extend themselves can help to make visits more meaningful.

One father said that the nicest birthday present he ever received was his son's offer to spend a day with him doing whatever the father wanted. Children who spend an allotted time with one parent find that such offers help to convert a "Disneyland Dad" into a better one.

JOINT CUSTODY

Karen is a 50-50 child—50 percent of the time is spent in her mother's home and 50 percent of the time in her father's. Someone asked her if she felt like a ping-pong ball. Actually, Karen's joint custody arrangement is working out very well with half a week in two different apartments that are just three miles apart. She keeps a separate set of clothing at each of the two homes, she follows two sets of rules for watching television, getting to bed, and so forth, but she has one school and one set of friends. Karen is glad that her parents love her enough to let her love both of them and to spend part of her time with each of them. She gives all her friends her schedule and both telephone numbers, so they know where to reach her all the time. In some ways, having two homes is fun for Karen.

Joint custody is not always so practical. For example, if parents live far from each other, or if there is no bedroom for a child in one home, such an arrangement can be difficult, if not impossible. Some children spend six months with one parent and six months with the other. Much of the success of sharing custody depends on the ability of parents to put aside their post-divorce resentments.

Consider the case of Jill and Bob. Their parents had been divorced two years ago and their mother had been awarded custody. Then their father decided he wanted to see them for more than their usual short visits, and he applied for a change in their custody arrangement, asking for joint custody. Their mother viewed their father as a gambler and an inattentive father who abused his children. He described himself as a devoted and responsible father. He assessed their mother as a woman who hung around bars, picked up men, and brought them home for the night. She described herself as a homebody.

No matter who was right, such a joint custody request would be refused. According to judges and specialists who favor joint custody, it can only be helpful to the children when the parents do not harbor ill feelings toward each other. These parents were so embittered that they could not be expected to make responsible decisions while sharing the physical custody of their children.

The success of joint custody depends on the ability of parents to bury their hostilities and separate their feelings for their children from their feelings for each other. One couple who had an unfriendly divorce had a seven-year custody battle that was resolved by a joint custody arrangement, which appeared to be an unlikely solution at the time. The daughter was six months old when the parents separated. For the next seven years, the girl's mother had denied visitation rights to the father many times and the father had taken the matter to court many times. The girl, who is eight, now lives with each parent for half the week and seems much happier. Even her mother, who was against the new arrangement at the beginning, admits that the child has stopped stuttering and twitching. There seems no doubt that the best interests of the child were served in this case.

Since joint custody means the sharing of the major responsibilities for rearing and caring for the children as well as for making everyday decisions, there are times when it has proven both difficult and dangerous. For example, one child was placed in a difficult position when a mother wanted to send him to a certain school and the father blocked this by legal action. In another case, the parents could not agree on whether or not to allow a surgical operation.

CHILDREN AS A WEAPON

Unfortunately the hostility between parents can be so great that they may use their child in a spiteful way. Linda's mother was badly hurt when her husband chose to move out of the house to live with another woman. Even though Linda was only three at the time, she had a very close relationship with her father and she missed his daily attention and warmth.

Linda's mother loved her, but something as minor as a glass of spilled milk could cause a scene that was followed by severe punishment. Her mother felt that the little girl was always making a mess in the house and the chores seemed endless. She seldom spent any time enjoying Linda; she was far more concerned with how the child was dressed and how she could prevent her from cluttering the house.

Although Linda's mother was awarded sole custody, her father had visiting rights and he came to see his daughter as often as he could. Her mother resented these visits so much that she spoke to her lawyer about trying to stop them. She claimed that the father frightened the child. This was one way she could punish her husband for the way he had left them. An evaluation was suggested before the parents' lawyers brought the case before a judge so that therapists could determine whether or not the claim that Linda's father frightened Linda was really true. The mother insisted the child could not sleep after the father had visited and this was due to the way he upset her. The father claimed that Linda enjoyed his visits and benefited from them.

Since Linda was not old enough to enter into any discussion of her feelings, it was decided to place the child in a room all by herself for a brief time. The therapists could observe her from the next room through a panel of glass that made them invisible.

Linda's mother and father entered the room at separate times. When her mother appeared, the therapist saw that she continued to play with the dolls in the doll house. When her mother left and her father entered the room, Linda ran to him and threw her arms around him. Certainly, this contradicted the kind of relationship that the mother had described.

Later, a psychiatrist asked Linda to play with the dolls in a doll house. There was a mother doll, a father doll, and a little girl. As she played, Linda placed the little girl with the father and kept the mother in a different part of the house.

On the basis of these sessions, further tests, and discussions, Linda's mother was persuaded to permit the child's relationship with her father to continue. Through a long period of therapy, her mother was helped to relate to Linda in a more positive way and to understand that the sleepless nights after the father's visits might be due partly to her own feelings of anxiety and hostility that were picked up by her daughter.

CHILDREN AS AN EGO TRIP

Paul hated his visits with his father, but he was made to spend every other weekend at his father's house. Actually, he never really felt that he was spending time with his father. His father would take him along to his club where Paul would swim and read while his father played golf. At the end of the day, they would go back to his father's house where Paul would eat some fried chicken or a hamburger from the take-out store down the street. His father would dress for dinner while Paul was eating, and then he would either go out or entertain some adults, leaving Paul to watch television alone. The next day's routine was much the same, with each person going his own way.

Paul often tried to arrange to stay home with his friends rather than spend the weekend at his father's house, but his father refused to give up the arrangement at his home. Paul couldn't see what difference it made to his father. He never suspected his father took pride in his power to keep Paul away from his former wife when she wanted her son at home.

CHILDREN AS SPIES

Don was uncomfortable about going from one parent to the other because both parents used him as a spy. When he was with his mother, she inquired about what his father did in his new living quarters. She was curious about how he spent his free time, whether or not he was dating any women, what they were like, and how much money he spent on them. Don's father asked questions about his mother's friends, how much she drank and smoked, and where she slept. Don tried to please each parent by giving as many answers as he could, but he felt as if he was always in the middle. Besides, he did not really like himself for spying. Actually, his parents were using him to help continue their fighting. When Don asked the school counselor what he could do about this, she suggested that he refuse to answer questions about the other parent. She told him that no one respects a spy since such a person cannot be trusted with a secret.

Don found that after he took a firm stand with each parent several times, the questions stopped. He felt much better about both parents and about himself when the spying stopped.

CUSTODY FIGHTS

Judy's parents were divorced when she was seven years old and she was placed in the custody of her mother, who lived in New York State. By choice, she spent summers with her father in Vermont. When she was nine years old, Judy's father decided not to send her back to her mother in time for school and fight for the custody of his daughter.

Judy's mother tried to contact her without success. No one would answer her questions when she called the father's house. She was referred to her former husband's lawyer. No one consulted Judy about whether or not she wanted to go back to her mother and the school she had attended the year before. Her father just decided he wanted to keep her with him. He took the case to court and filed legal papers claiming that his wife was not a fit mother because she was under the constant care of a psychiatrist, even though this was untrue. Judy was enrolled in a school near her father's home and entered the first day of the fall term just as if she would be staying for the full year.

In the meantime, Judy's mother hired a lawyer who issued a warrant for the arrest of Judy's father. This was possible because he had interfered with the custody order that was issued at the time of the divorce in New York. However, the warrant was useless at that date unless her father appeared in New York since out-of-state custody orders did not then apply in Vermont.

Judy's mother, who was not at all unfit to care for the child as her former husband had claimed, was told by her lawyer to go to Vermont and take Judy home with her. But her mother worried: what would this do to Judy? Her mother did drive to the school and she checked with the principal to see if her daughter was really attending school and inquired whether her daughter was well. Since this appeared to be true, the mother returned home to await the court hearing.

Two months elapsed. At last, the hearing came before a judge. Judy's mother did not see her daughter in the courthouse where she had been brought by her father's lawyer until Judy took the stand and was asked to choose between her parents. The father had already tried to persuade Judy to choose him. The judge, who refused to allow a nine-year-old to choose between two hostile parents, took the girl to his chambers where he had a private conversation with the disturbed child. He had already read the report on the father's allegation that the mother was unfit and learned that it was untrue. Two weeks later, Judy's mother was notified that the judge upheld the New York decree and that she could take her daughter home with her permanently.

Although Judy was glad to return to her old home and school, she felt confused by the whole experience. Even though her father had been wrong, she would miss her summer visits with him. In Judy's case, as in most custody fights, the child is the big loser.

If the Uniform Child Custody Act had been in effect in all states when Judy's parents were fighting for her custody, her father would not have been able to keep her away so long. States that ratify this act honor the orders of any other state where child custody matters are concerned. By the spring of 1981, most states had made this part of their laws.

An increasing number of families are working out custody problems with the help of people who are impartial. In Los Angeles, California, a conciliation court solves about 55 percent of the cases. Therapists, employed by the court, do custody evaluations, and custody investigators do family studies, and interview teachers, neighbors, and friends to help determine the living arrangement that is best for each child. In many different states, a guardian is appointed for a child in an effort to represent the child's point of view and to be objective in the emotional times of determining the best custody situation. In Wisconsin, the court is required by law to appoint an attorney for the child in a contested custody case.

Fortunately, most parents are able to resolve the problems of custody without seriously draining their financial and emotional resources on court battles. About 90 percent of child custody arrangements are settled without serious court battles in which a judge has to decide the question of who gets custody of the children. One hopes that in all cases the needs of the children are a primary consideration.

PARENTAL KIDNAPPING

A growing number of parents are snatching their children from the parent who has custody and fleeing with them to far places. Some of the true stories of parental kidnapping sound like spy stories. Parents and children have been known to escape the custodial parent by flying away in light engine planes, using false passports to hide in foreign countries, bribing foreign bureaucrats, and using elaborate disguises.

Sometimes, a young child who has been kidnapped by a parent is unaware of what has happened, at least for the first few weeks. This was the case for David, a four-year-old boy whose Italian father was an international businessman. David thought the flight from New York to Rome with his father was the beginning of a vacation in which he would spend some time with his father's family in Italy. As the weeks stretched on, David began to realize that this was not just a vacation.

His mother, an attorney in New York, started court proceedings which led to the return of the boy in four and a half months. Not all children are returned this fast and some never go back to the parent from which they were stolen.

As many as 100,000 children are believed to be kidnapped by parents every year in the United States alone. Many are taken across state lines and an increasing number are being taken across national boundaries. Mrs. Rodriguez was living in California when her former husband took their eight-year-old twins to Argentina. This mother sold her house and borrowed $250,000 to pay lawyers and detectives to help get the children away from their father. She went to Argentina, and three years after he took them, a judge in Argentina signed the order which permitted Mrs. Rodriguez to take them back to the United States. She and the boys fled in a small plane immediately for fear the father would file an appeal that would detain the children.

Very few people can afford the fees for detectives and lawyers in a private search for their stolen children. The police seldom help when cases are reported to them because it is difficult to prove that there is a crime when the children are taken by a parent. Even the FBI cannot help in many child-snatching cases. However, there have been cases in which people without a great deal of money have been able to locate and rescue their children. Ruth Livingston's case was one of these.

Mrs. Livingston lived in California with her toddlers, Jimmy and Sally. She had worked out an arrangement with another mother of young children to look after them while she worked. Although she was not legally divorced from her husband, she had started the proceedings and had asked for custody of the children. She tried to keep her whereabouts secret because her husband had been abusive to her. The father managed to find her, however, and to steal the children by forcing his way into the place where they were living. He had two friends pose as police officers who demanded that the children go with their father. The baby-sitter who was staying with the children was so frightened and confused that the father had a two-hour start before the mother was located. Even then, the police could not have arrested him since he was the children's father and there had been no broken custody agreement.

Eighteen months went by. During this time, Mrs. Livingston did not know where her children were or whether they were safe and healthy. Then she had a lead about where the children might be. As a result of an application she made out for a loan at the bank, she discovered that her husband had overdrawn money from a joint account that she had shared with him. The bank had traced him to a city in Texas. The telephone company had been able to give her his phone number, so she dialed his number, heard his voice, and hung up without telling him who she was. Things began to happen fast. The next day, her divorce was granted and she was given custody of the children. And the following day, Mrs. Livingston and her father drove to the city in Texas where her husband was living. Here she learned that neither the police nor the local district attorney's office would help, but they promised not to stop her from taking the children back home with her. After a period of confusion, the children were happily on their way back to their former home in California with their mother, who had the legal right to care for them.

Although childnapping by a father appears to be more common than by a mother, there are many cases in which a mother takes the children illegally. In either type of situation, the problems usually take a long time to resolve. For example, one mother of a two-year-old disappeared with her daughter after she lost custody to the father because she refused to let him visit the child. It was two years later when the father succeeded in bringing his child back from a neighboring state.

What causes parental kidnapping? In many cases, child snatching occurs because one parent refuses to allow the other to visit the child. Sometimes a parent feels that the other parent is making unfair financial demands. The feeling that judges are unfair in awarding children to the custody of mothers on the basis of sex is thought to be behind some of the cases of parental kidnapping. The consequences hurt the parents and children no matter what the motives. In one tragic case, a father and son were killed in a car crash when they were being chased by the child's mother.

Few people can appreciate the extent of the emotional damage to children who are kidnapped by parents, and hidden under the cover of their moving from place to place. They live constantly in a tension-filled situation, which sometimes lasts for years. In one case, two children were taken by their mother from their father in Michigan. The mother settled with them in New York where the father located them and appealed to the court. They lived with their mother for three years, during which court appeals moved slowly through the legal process. In the end, they moved back to

Michigan and were in the custody of their father, but during the time they were gone, both the children and their old environment had changed a great deal.

Perhaps you are wondering why someone doesn't do something to help the many children and parents who are victims of child snatching. Many children who have been kidnapped report that they feel something like baggage being carried from city to city. They never stay long in one school or home, so they never really have a chance to make serious friendships. These children are often coerced to use aliases, live under the guard of detectives, and lie to authorities. Many of the children suffer great emotional pain in longing for the parent from whom they have been taken. So even though parental kidnapping may not seem serious to law enforcement agencies, it is both serious and tragic for those directly involved. With rare exceptions, parental kidnapping is a destructive act on the part of the parent who does the kidnapping.

In the closing hours of the 96th Congress, a measure to deter child snatching passed without debate and was signed into law by President Carter during Christmas week of 1980. The new law orders the Federal Bureau of Investigation to use its resources to help locate parents who have taken their children across state lines after arrest warrants have been issued. It also increases cooperation between states. Formerly some had refused to cooperate with each other on custody cases unless children were in physical danger.

Some organizations act as clearinghouses for parents whose children are kidnapped or hidden from them by other parents. One of these, Children's Rights, Inc. is a national nonprofit organization seeking a solution to the problems of child-snatching and child restraint. Only a small percentage of the children in their files have been found. On the basis of many cases, the leaders of this group estimate that if the children are not found within six months, they probably will not be found for years.

One mother who reported her story in the newsletter published by Children's Rights, Inc. said that her two girls had been kidnapped in March 1974. Her former husband, after telling her that he was taking the girls on a shopping trip, boarded a plane with them and flew to Bombay, India, where he had lived earlier. The mother followed and was able to get custody rights, but before she could take the children back to the United States, the father fled with them to Iran. Strict paternal custody laws in that country made it impossible for the mother to get them back from Iran, but she was able to obtain pictures of the girls in 1975 through the help of the United States Embassy. In 1980, she discovered that the children and her husband had left Iran two years earlier and had returned to the United States. At the time of the report, she was still trying to locate the children and obtain custody.

In an effort to help children and the parents from whom they have been kidnapped, the Special Commission on Child Abduction of the Hague Conference (an international group) is working toward a treaty among the twenty-two subscribing countries. The formation of an International Task Force would assist in the return of children snatched across international borders.

At present, the Passport Office of the United States will cooperate with parents who file descriptive information about their missing children and furnish a restraining order on the Passport Office. In this way, parents can, to a degree, protect their children from being taken out of the country against their wishes, but some slip by under different names.

Many parents worked together to help change the federal kidnapping statutes, but there are still many heartaches for the victims of parental kidnapping. Children's Rights, Inc. has been receiving over fifteen calls every day from parents who are seeking children who have been snatched away from them. No one knows how many parental kidnappings take place each year. Efforts to prevent child snatching will be important until this experience is no longer a threat to any children.

5

LIVING IN STEPFAMILIES

Cindy sat glowering on the steps of the house belonging to the man her mother had married and watched the empty moving van drive away. She really hated this house, even though her desk, her books, her bicycle, and most of her other possessions were in this place that was to be her new home. She had her own room, a room that was larger than the one in the old house, but it would never be the same. She missed her friends, her old school, the park where she used to play, and just about everything.

"Hello," a friendly voice interrupted her musing. A short, stout woman stood in front of her. "Are you Mr. King's new little girl?" the woman inquired. Cindy shook her head to say no, even though she knew that Mr. King was now her stepfather. He could never replace her father, Cindy was sure. She would never be his little girl.

Cindy was just one of many children who experience hostility when parents remarry. They see the stepparent as a permanent intrusion in their relationship with their remaining natural parent and as an end to the hope that their divorced parents might someday remarry. Cindy was not one of the fortunate children who could talk with her stepfather about her feelings. Her stepfather did not know how to make her understand that he would not compete with her father, or to explain how his place in her life would be unique and different from the relationship with her own father. He knew he was an additional parent, and did not think he was a replacement. Nor did her mother.

Many families enter into stepfamily relationships with the idea that the family relationships will be the same or fall into place as in their original families. They are optimistic, but they are unaware of the many different feelings that must be resolved.

About fifty million people in the United States live in stepfamilies, families that differ in many ways from the biological family into which most children are born. All these individuals come together with ghosts from the past, with good ways and bad ways of doing and feeling. Most come with mixed feelings about their new situations.

Suppose you are getting another mother as a result of your father's remarriage. Technically, she is your stepmother, but you don't call her that when you speak to her. Just finding the most comfortable name for this new member of your family can be a problem, and society has not really provided a good solution. You probably do not want to call her mother, especially if your own mother is alive. But you might feel comfortable with a variation of the name you use for your own mother. You might call her by her first name. This is one solution that is common, but there are some stepmothers who feel that this puts them in a bad position when there is a need to discipline. Many stepmothers are called aunt along with their first names. Others like to be called Mom Joan, or a similar combination of a name for mother and their own names. As mentioned earlier, even stepfamilies are called by many names, such as blended families, reconstituted families, and reorganized families.

THE CRUEL STEPMOTHER MYTH

The whole idea of a stepmother comes with built-in problems, partly because of the stories that are told to young children. The stepmothers in legends and fairy tales have traditionally been wicked. For example, Cinderella's stepmother is well known for making her work at dirty tasks while the rest of the family goes to the ball. One young child was terrified of joining a stepfamily in which she would have two older stepsisters because she imagined herself being treated like Cinderella and she feared she might not find a happy ending as in the story.

Most children are familiar with other tales of cruel stepmothers such as the one in the story of "Snow White." Her beautiful stepmother was reassured each day that she was the most beautiful of all when she consulted her mirror. One day the mirror told her that her stepdaughter, Snow White, was now the fairest of all. The stepmother solved this problem by having Snow White taken out to the woods to be put to death. In the end, Snow White marries a handsome prince and her stepmother is the one who dies.

The stepmother in "Hansel and Gretel" is famous for her cruelty, too. When there was not enough food to go around, the stepchildren were sent away to fend for themselves in the woods. They kill the witch (who symbolizes the cruel stepmother) and return home to find that their stepmother has died.

In the story, "The Juniper Tree" the cruel stepmother cuts the stepchild into pieces for soup, and she serves it to the father, who eats it.

The myth of the cruel stepmother is one of the factors that makes a good relationship difficult. In real life, stories about stepmothers tend to be cruel, too. The great majority of stepmothers try very hard to be good in their new roles. Some of these, who are objects of hostility, are hindered because they try too hard.

THE MYTH OF INSTANT LOVE

Twelve-year-old Joan and her father felt very close after her mother had left them. They depended on each other as friends. Joan's first reaction was one of jealousy when her father's new wife, Barbara, came into the picture. Joan developed headaches when Barbara was around. Barbara, on the other hand, was very self-assured. She played games with Joan, took her shopping, and did many favors for her new stepdaughter. She was sure that she could win her over, but somehow she lacked sensitivity. Actually, Barbara tried so hard that she made things more difficult.

Barbara rearranged her own schedule to fit Joan's. She tried to anticipate the girl's needs and satisfy her wants even when they seemed unreasonable. Still Joan was resistant. Trying to be the perfect stepmother became exhausting for Barbara.

Joan did not appreciate Barbara's special efforts to please her, and Barbara got upset because she tried so hard and did not win her new daughter's love.

The myth of the cruel stepmother is no more prevalent than the myth of instant love. Many women who are about to become instant mothers to the children of the men they marry feel that they will be able to win the child's affection quickly. Sometimes this feeling is encouraged by good relationships before marriage. The father and his future wife go on outings with his children and have many enjoyable times. But it is typical for the good times to stop when the actual marriage takes place.

Experts who work with the problems of stepfamilies state again and again that it is unrealistic to expect stepchildren and stepparents to love each other immediately upon formation of the new family. Even the impression that they must love each other can be harmful. Just because a woman loves a man, it does not follow that she will immediately love his children. Even those children who think they love a person who is going to become a stepparent discover that living together is very different from sharing outings and good times at the movies. It takes a long time for love to grow between people even when there are no complicated feelings involved, as there are in the case of stepfamilies.

Stepparents and stepchildren find it helpful to know that they should not be expected to love each other immediately. The family can be happy as long as there is respect and consideration for each of the members. Both children and parents need time to adjust, accept, and belong. Love is often a bonus that comes later.

LOYALTY

Loyalty is one of the feelings that gets in the way of a good relationship with a stepparent. Suppose the natural mother has died. The children remember her as a wonderful person. In fact, they tend to idealize her. This new mother can never replace their own mother, nor should she expect to replace her.

When Sue's father remarried, Sue assembled all the pictures she could find of her mother, who had died when Sue was four years old. Now that she was eight, Sue remembered only the happy days they had together. Actually, Sue's mother had been very depressed and she took her own life. Sue's father had never told Sue about this, for he wanted her to remember her early childhood days as happy and think of her mother as a caring person.

Sue's father was especially happy with his new wife, who was good humored and very easygoing. She tried to understand Sue's feelings of loyalty to her mother and helped the girl frame some of her mother's pictures. Even with this understanding, it took many years before Sue could feel close to this new mother. On some days, she felt that she hated her father for neglecting the memory of her mother. But on other days, she felt contented to be close to a mature, older woman who could listen to her problems and care for her needs.

When a natural mother dies, psychologists believe that the children harbor some resentment toward her for having abandoned them, even though they are aware of the fact that in the majority of cases she had no control over her death. Since this hostility cannot be expressed openly, the stepmother may serve as a target for it.

When a mother and a stepmother are both part of a child's family, loyalties can be difficult, too. There is naturally some rivalry between the biological mother and the stepmother for the children's affection. The natural mother resents the actions of the stepmother, no matter how well intentioned they may be. The children are put in a position of divided loyalty, and they usually side with their natural mothers. They feel guilty if they like or love their stepmothers. When children realize that some of their problems in relating to their stepmothers are partly due to these loyalty conflicts, their hostile feelings are usually less strong. Children need to be reminded again and again that their relationship with stepparents is different from the relationship with natural parents. Stepparents do not replace the natural parent, but act as additional parents.

SHARING A PARENT

Having a new stepparent means sharing a natural parent. Many children feel that the stepparent is going to take the love of their parent away completely, so they will lose the only remaining parent. For some children, remarriage means losing one's place as an only child or losing a position in the family as the eldest or the youngest child. It is easier if children can express the anxieties and doubts that are felt when a stepparent enters the family. Everyone has some of these feelings, for there are changes with which everyone must cope.

Before her mother remarried, Kim felt that she had a very special place in her mother's life. Now, her stepfather took a great deal of her mother's free time. Kim decided to go to her room every day when she came home from school and she refused to eat dinner at the table with her stepfather. Kim was sullen and withdrawn, isolating herself from the family in every possible way. She continued this behavior for several months. She knew that she was jealous of her stepfather, but she did not realize that part of the problem was anger at her mother for having betrayed her by bringing this new person into the family, and fear that she would lose her special place in her mother's heart to her stepfather. It was almost a year before Kim began to accept her stepfather and find that there was room for this additional person. Eventually she discovered that he even added some good things to her life.

WE DO IT THIS WAY HERE

At some time or other most stepmothers hear the words, "You are not my mother. You have no right to tell me what to do."

When his wife died, Mr. Blair retired so that he could take care of his three teenage daughters. He devoted all of his time to cooking for them, transporting them to their activities, and providing for their needs. He grew more and more lonesome as the girls grew older and spent an increasing amount of their time with their friends. Gradually, Mr. Blair formed a good relationship with a woman. This woman, whose name was Barbara, had been divorced for a long time. He and Barbara decided to marry and Barbara moved into the Blair home.

The girls disliked sharing their father with his new wife but they tried to accept Barbara as an older friend and as a member of the family. They found this very difficult after having their father to themselves. Barbara felt that her new husband waited on the girls too much. They were used to having him serve the meals and clean up afterward. Now Barbara was serving the meals, but she expected the girls to do the dishes, and she told them so. They reacted by telling her that she had no right to give them orders. Unfortunately, their father did not support Barbara in her request, but he helped her with the chores she asked the girls to do. Mealtime conversation consisted of asking for the salt or a second helping of food. Barbara, who thought she would enjoy having company at meal-time after living alone for many years, felt very frustrated in her attempts to make pleasant con-versation.

If Mr. Blair had discussed the rules of the house with Barbara before they were married and sup-ported her in some of her requests, the marriage would have been more pleasant for everyone.

In many families, there is confusion because children live with two sets of parents and find that there are two sets of rules. In the Russell house-hold, the stepmother responds to "My mother does it this way," with "In this house, we do it differ-ently." For example, bedtime is 11 P.M. at the nat-ural mother's house and 10 P.M. at the Russell house. Mrs. Russell holds firm to her rules, insist-ing that in this house the children go to bed at 10 P.M. The same holds true about chores, mealtime rules, and picking up clothing. Mrs. Russell knows that the children feel more secure when they know what is expected of them and that someone cares enough to see that they follow the rules of the house.

Many stepparents feel timid about disciplining children who are not theirs, while others plunge in with extremely rigid rules. It helps if they are aware of the need to be flexible and understanding.

KINDS OF LOVE

Many stepparents grow to love the children from former marriages as much as they would ever love children who were born to them. In some cases, where a natural parent shows no interest in a child, adoption seems to be a happy arrangement for all the people involved.

One stepfather who had adopted his wife's daughter by a former marriage fought the Unification Church for five years because he claimed that they had exercised mind control techniques in recruiting her and depriving him of his natural parental rights. This stepfather volunteered that he was willing to "give up everything" to get his adopted daughter back from the church group she had chosen to live with instead of her family.

Sometimes children are appalled to discover that they may stimulate their new stepparents or stepbrothers or stepsisters sexually if they wander around the house in various stages of undress as has been their custom.

One stepfather found that he felt very uncomfortable when his stepdaughters continued to live as casually as they had before he joined the family. He suggested that the girls wear robes when they were not fully dressed and that they all respect each other's privacy. Sometimes a stepfather and stepdaughter are attracted to each other in a sexual way. This situation is often helped by a professional therapist.

Many cases of runaway girls involve stepfathers who sexually abuse them. Most stepfathers are not guilty of this kind of behavior, but if you feel uneasy about a situation of this kind, discuss it with your own parent. If this does not lead to the help you need, contact a local mental health center or other place in the list of suggestions at the end of this book.

STEPBROTHERS AND STEPSISTERS

Many children of remarried parents find themselves sharing a house with brothers and sisters who are children of the stepparent. In one household where the parents had combined their furniture and dishes, the children showed definite preference for the things that had come from their original houses. In all cases, people bring old habits and behavior from their previous family life. Sometimes, ways of doing things cause conflicts, and it helps if the family can realize that everyone has to make adjustments.

Jealousy is common in families where the children are "his" and "hers," and in the cases where there are new children by the remarriage. Often a father feels guilty because he spends more time with his stepchildren than with his own children because of the living arrangement. When stepbrothers and stepsisters live together, there is often jealousy about favoritism of a natural parent, or over attention paid to stepchildren. Few families blend as easily as on the popular television shows, where all the problems seem to be solved during a half-hour program.

Many stepfamilies work out their difficulties by discussing roles and rules at family conferences. Each one tries to put himself or herself in the shoes of everyone else involved in the stepfamily relationship and to understand how the other members of the family are feeling. This is not easy. Instant families seldom find instant harmony, but it helps to know that people in stepfamilies have special feelings and that they need not feel guilty about many of the negative ones.

In most stepfamilies, people are happier if they understand that stepfamilies are different from natural families and that everyone has to try a little harder. Children who can discuss their feelings have an easier time making room for three or four parents in their lives. Although there are times when stepchildren are lonely, and unhappy about the divorce of their parents, many of them are able to find good things about having a stepparent.

6

FEELING BETTER ABOUT YOURSELF

How you value yourself plays an important part in what happens to you. No one feels good all of the time, but some people have an overall feeling of worth that helps them face all kinds of obstacles courageously. They trust themselves and they expect to be successful. Their expectations color their behavior and they are eager, outgoing, and confident—apt to be winners.

Many people feel that they are worthless and see themselves as losers. They do not feel self-assured in any situation so they are guarded in their actions. This kind of behavior, in which people expect to fail, makes failure more likely. For example, tennis players know that their games are better on days when they feel good about themselves. When there is tension and a feeling of being no good, the chances of losing are greater. This is true in sports and in many everyday situations, too.

Even people who feel self-confident most of the time do not always feel good about themselves, but Jerry never felt good about himself. He insisted that his father would not have left the family if Jerry had not argued with him at his birthday dinner. That was when his father left the table with the remark that he had had enough of the family and went to live with someone else in a nearby town. No matter how hard his mother tried, she could not convince Jerry that his defiance was only a trigger that set something in motion that had been present for a long time. Jerry was always one who felt that he was worthless even before the divorce. He felt that his parents' arguments were all over him, although most of them really were not. The memory of bitter battles made him afraid, and held him back from making overtures of friendship to other people. Although he tried a few times, he was positive he would fail, and he did. Jerry spent many sad years feeling sorry for himself because his parents were divorced.

"What can you expect? He comes from a broken home." This kind of remark is usually meant to be unflattering but this may not always be so. Divorce is leaving fewer emotional scars now than it used to. So many of today's children who grow up in homes where parents are separated are facing up to the extra stresses so well that people are taking a new look at the situation.

Over one million children are involved in their parents' divorces every year. Many of these children spend an unusual amount of time questioning their own worth and endure periods that are especially difficult, but in time they show that they can do just as well as those who grow up in families that are intact with the original parents. For these children of divorced parents, the divorce, in time, means only a memory of an unhappy year of childhood.

Rather than feeling sorry for themselves, many children of divorce recognize the fact that they are not as lucky as most children who are born to parents who continue to love each other. There are children, also, whose parents are still living together who are no luckier or happier than children whose parents have separated. In both kinds of families there are some children who do not feel good about themselves and indeed would not in any situation.

WHAT IS SELF-ESTEEM?

Feeling good about oneself is known as self-esteem. A person with good self-esteem is not a conceited person, but one who has a quiet sense of self-respect.

"Mary really thinks she is somebody special," says a boy who thinks she is conceited. Actually, Mary is wearing a mask of noisy conceit. Inside, she feels unlovable but she hides her feelings by appearing self-confident and perfect. She works to appear this way, using her energy to seem confident rather than being so. Still, there are people who recognize that she is just a little too uppity and that her gestures are too exaggerated. They know that she is hiding her feelings of worthlessness behind this mask of conceit. She is using one of the many unhealthy defenses that hide inadequacy.

Psychologists and psychiatrists associate self-esteem and self-confidence with potential for happiness. The person who is trying hard to impress people has less time and energy for more productive activities and recreation. People with low self-esteem restrict their lives because they do not have the courage to risk new experiences.

If your self-esteem is high, you are glad you are you. You do not waste energy trying to impress others because you know you have value. You can use that energy in more valuable ways, knowing that you have something to offer others.

DIVORCE AND SELF-ESTEEM

Many things connected with divorce can contribute to lowering a child's self-esteem. For example, most parents who are separating are deeply involved with new burdens. They may give children the feeling that they are an added economic hardship, that they interfere with a career, that they interfere with a parent's future relationships with the opposite sex, and so on. A child may sense this and develop a lower sense of self-worth. Some children are used as the target for a parent who feels resentment toward a husband or wife. Jennifer was such a case.

Jennifer's father was easily irritated over little mannerisms, such as the way she tossed her hair because this reminded him of his wife, who had left him for another man. When Jennifer visited her father, he often commented that she was just like her mother. It was hard for Jennifer to accept the fact that her father's hostility was really directed against her mother and not against her. His treatment did not help her to feel good about herself.

If stepparents or one of your parents makes hostile remarks about your other parent, try to recognize the fact that you are a constant reminder of a part of life that was unpleasant. When parents are tearing down one another, they do not realize that their children usually have a profound loyalty for both parents and that they are struggling to preserve that loyalty.

Some children suffer because a parent uses the child as a substitute for a missing husband or wife. Such a child feels anxious because he or she cannot provide advice and comfort that only an adult is equipped to handle. Of course, the child does not realize this, but the result is a lowering of the child's self-esteem.

Many children suffer because the behavior of a missing parent was especially bad. For example, Joe's father was an alcoholic who beat the boy's mother whenever he was very drunk. Joe not only suffered from the problems at home, but his classmates were no help. They taunted him with remarks about his father. They asked Joe if he was going to be a wife-beater or if he could handle his beer better than his father. Joe felt the stigma to the point of becoming shy and hating himself. Only with long-term professional help was he able to see that he did not contribute in any way to his father's behavior and that he should not blame himself for it. He was helped to realize that the people who ridiculed him had problems with their own behavior and it was they who should feel a-shamed of themselves. Joe found it difficult to realize that he was just unlucky in having a father who behaved the way he did, and that this did not make *him* bad and he would not necessarily grow up to be like his father. Eventually, Joe found that people liked him for himself, in spite of his father's reputation.

Through his many talks with the therapist, Joe learned something about his father that he had not been able to understand. From all he saw and heard, his father seemed like a really bad person. Certainly, his father's behavior was bad. However, Joe learned that his father had grown up in a family that was always putting him down, so he had a very bad opinion of himself. The man's early experiences convinced him that he was of little or no worth, for no matter how hard he tried he could not earn his parent's love. Frustrated by his inability to gain any satisfaction, his father began to withdraw from the world at an early age in a self-destructive way. When he was upset, he drank until he no longer felt anxious. By the time Joe was born, his father was addicted to alcohol to the degree that there were chemical changes in his body that made him crave it. He had also learned to release some of his hate by striking out at people who crossed him. Unfortunately, Joe's mother was often the target.

Although Joe's father's problems were very complicated and he would never fully understand them, Joe could at least realize that his father was not just a bad man and that Joe himself did not come from "bad stock."

BUILDING SELF-ESTEEM

Fortunately, one's self-esteem can change. A person who thinks he or she is worthless can find messages from a variety of people that help in building better self-esteem.

Paul felt that he was a real disappointment to his father and his stepmother. He tried to bulldoze his way to acceptance by fighting and acting cool, but he really felt small and worthless inside. His search for a way to count in the eyes of his friends led him to the leadership of a gang that vandalized the school. Vandalizing the school got him prestige and attention from authorities, albeit negative attention. Since Paul felt he was no good, he thought he might just as well act that way. But, fortunately, Paul's behavior improved when one of his teachers took a special interest in him.

One day, Paul was playing basketball after school, and the coach noticed that he excelled in making baskets. He persuaded Paul to join the school team. Even though Paul did not want to be ridiculed by his gang of friends, he knew that he did not really like himself for the trouble he was making. He had to stay at school to sweep the basketball court anyhow as part of his punishment for breaking school windows. Since he had to wait until practice was over, he thought he might as well join the group.

Even though excelling in basketball helped to build Paul's self-esteem, this was not the most important factor in his changed opinion of himself. The coach of the team was trained to help people who were having problems at home and in school. Paul felt that he was appreciated by the coach, who encouraged him and praised his strengths rather than dwelling on his bad behavior.

After some success in making new friends, Paul began to like himself better. He liked himself well enough to know that he did not have to be perfect. When his parents pointed out his shortcomings, he did not give into them. He had enough positive feelings with other people and from other experiences to feel competent and worthwhile.

Perhaps you feel that an unhappy childhood has ruined your life. Not everyone is as fortunate as Paul, but everyone can help himself or herself to feel less worthless.

According to the research of some psychologists, a happy childhood is not the key to adult happiness. Professor Jonathan Freedman of Columbia University conducted a survey that indicated the influence of childhood on happiness is weaker than many people have concluded in the past. Many people whose parents died or were divorced, who were treated coldly, and who led unhappy childhoods, Professor Freedman found, still manage to be very happy as adults. The one factor that carries over from childhood to adulthood is guilt and with guilt comes a feeling of self-loathing. Therefore, it is especially important for children of divorce to realize that they are not the cause of the divorce and that parents are divorcing each other, not the children.

Self-esteem has been called the key to inner peace and happy living, but suppose you think you are unlovable and not worthwhile. Is it too late to do something about it?

Fortunately, people can raise their self-esteem no matter what their ages. The feeling of worth has to be learned, so the feeling of worthlessness can be unlearned. People can grow and change all their lives, so they can learn to feel better about themselves.

One way to begin building self-esteem is to make a self-inventory. How aware are you of your special qualities? Since there is no other person in the world exactly like you, you have some capacities and strengths that are special to you. You can make yourself more aware of these, and develop and enjoy them more. Perhaps you think you have no special qualities that make you worthwhile. What about being a good listener? The world needs good listeners, but many people's lives are too cluttered with mental trash to hear what others are saying. Children often complain that their parents never listen to them. This may be true because many people do not know how to listen.

You can begin to be a good listener by listening to two other people talking. Did either one hear the other person's point of view or was each person too busy trying to get his or her own message across? Did either person give concrete evidence that a message was received?

Now try listening to someone in your own family. When someone tells you about certain feelings, reflect about this and then try to understand from that person's point of view. For example, suppose your stepmother tells you that she is tired of driving you and your sister to school, to your friends' houses, to your music lesson, or to other places where you must be taken and picked up. At first, you might think that it is her job to drive you or that it isn't your fault that she has to do this, but try to consider her point of view. Try responding to her in a way that shows you understand how she feels. If you tell her that you can see that all this driving must be a problem for her, she knows you have heard her. You have been a good listener. You are helping her by listening.

Being a good listener, painting, singing, helping others, trying to understand others, playing games for fun but resisting the temptation to manipulate people, and an almost endless number of other things can help you to feel better about yourself. Just knowing that you can feel better is a good beginning. Just knowing that you are not trapped because your parents have separated or remarried, but that you are just one of millions of others who have had this kind of bad luck can help.

Joining a group of people who have had similar family experiences can be extremely helpful. In Lexington, Massachusetts, teenagers of divorced parents have formed a self-help group under the name of Divorced Kids Group in which they sort out feelings and give each other support. This group meets weekly under the supervision of a high school guidance counselor. Other groups in schools and community centers throughout the United States bring together people with similar problems. There may be such a group in your area, or you may want to ask an advisor to help you start this kind of a group.

The program for young people that is sponsored by the organization Parents Without Partners was mentioned on page 43 of this book. Remember, anyone can join the International Youth Council if they are between the ages of twelve and seventeen and their parents are separated, divorced, widowed, or never married.

Other organizations where you may find companionship and support are listed on pages 105-109. Many of the members of these groups come from single-parent homes or live in stepfamilies. Such groups help you to meet others who feel the same as you do. It helps to know that you are not the only one who harbors some bad thoughts and feelings and that you are not alone in trying to cope with important aspects of family life. These groups can help you to develop self-respect.

If you do not treat yourself with respect, you cannot expect others to do so. If you play the game of running yourself down, you can expect this kind of treatment from others. But if you are friendly and loving to yourself, you can do more to nurture others.

Do you tolerate your own mistakes? Remember, you can discard that which is unfitting and replace it with something better. You are living in the present and everything about you belongs to you. You can learn to see the glass of water half full along with optimists rather than half empty along with the pessimists, and to see the good in yourself.

Perhaps you will find it helpful to make a list each evening of the good things that happened to you and the good things you did during the day. Many people who do this learn to concentrate on the good things and find that they like themselves better.

Liking yourself better may be especially hard when you are feeling that a parent or stepparent dislikes you, but you can be aware that such feelings may be colored by complicated emotions that involve others. Although divorce can be a blow to self-esteem in many ways, the blow need not do permanent damage. You can help it heal.

7

WHERE TO GET HELP

If you cannot locate a local group of one of the following organizations, write to the national headquarters listed below to find out if there is a branch near you. You will find companionship when you join and a chance to develop new interests. You will probably find many members whose parents have been divorced. For example, according to one estimate, 44 percent of the members of the Boys' Clubs of America come from single-parent homes.

Big Brothers of America, 220 Suburban Station Building, Philadelphia, Pennsylvania 19103

Big Sisters International, 225 Suburban Station Building, Philadelphia, Pennsylvania 19103

Boys' Clubs of America, 771 First Avenue, New York, New York 10017

Boy Scouts of America, U.S. Highway Number 1, North Brunswick, New Jersey 08902

Camp Fire Girls, Inc., 1740 Broadway, New York, New York 10019

Girl Scouts of the U.S.A., 830 Third Avenue, New York, New York 10022

National 4-H Foundation, 7100 Connecticut Avenue, Washington, D.C. 20015

Parents Without Partners, International Youth Council, 7910 Woodmont Avenue, Washington, D.C. 20014

YMCA (Young Men's Christian Association), 291 Broadway, New York, New York 10007

YMHA (Young Men's Hebrew Association), 1395 Lexington Avenue, New York, New York, 10028

YWCA (Young Women's Christian Association) 600 Lexington Avenue, New York, New York 10022

YWHA (Young Women's Hebrew Association), 1395 Lexington Avenue, New York, New York 10028

For help with special kinds of problems:

If a parent is an *alcoholic,* contact Al-Anon Family Group Headquarters, P. O. Box 182, Madison Square Station, New York, New York 10010 to find out if there is a local Alateen group near you. One might be listed in your telephone book if you live in a large city.

If a parent has a *gambling* problem, contact Gam-Anon Family Groups, P. O. Box 248, Glassboro, New

Jersey 08028 to locate a Gamateen group near you.

If you are a *runaway* and want to let your parents know that you are safe, you can call either of the following numbers toll-free without identifying your location to your parents. Operators will help you to find shelter or to get home again if that is what you wish.

National Runaway Switchboard, 1-800-621-4000
Nationwide
1-800-972-6004 in
Illinois

Operation Peace of Mind 1-800-231-6946
Nationwide
1-800-231-6762 in
Alaska/Hawaii
1-800-392-3352 in Texas

If someone in your family has been or is in *prison* and you want to meet others whose parents have had the same experience, contact The Fortune Society, 29 East 22nd Street, New York, New York 10010

Short-term counseling helps many children of parents who have separated and remarried. In addition to help from school counselors, religious advisors, and medical doctors in general practice, some children are finding support from community and school programs such as the following. These serve as models for local groups:

Children of Divorce, Box 122, State College, Pennsylvania 16801 (Community based project)

Divorced Kids Group, Guidance Center, Lexington High School, Lexington, Massachusetts 02173 (High school program with emphasis on peer group support. Films available.)

Evergreen Developmental Center, P. O. Box 14, Evergreen, Colorado 80439 (Holds group sessions for parents and children, emphasizing problems of children after divorce)

Family Change Project, Minneapolis Public Schools, 711 11th Avenue, S.W., Minneapolis, Minnesota 55414 (School program)

Kids in the Middle, 8029 Forsyth Boulevard, Clayton, Missouri 63105, (Group sessions with parents and children of divorce)

The Divorce Experience, Domestic Relations Division, Hennepin County Family Court, Minneapolis, Minnesota 55487 (Family Court conducts sessions to help children and parents.)

If you want in-depth counseling:

Finding the person who can help you most may take

some searching because the quality of care varies and because each case is different. To find the services that best suit your needs, you can approach the following agencies. Most of them are listed in local telephone books.

Child Guidance Center

Community Mental Health Center

Mental Health Association of your area

Family or Youth Services of the Human Resources Department of your city or county

Outpatient psychiatric clinic of your local hospital (call the hospital)

American Psychiatric Association's local branch

American Psychological Association's local branch

Choose a therapist whose qualifications are licensed and who has had experience with your type of problem. You and your parents can inquire about qualifications and fees.

SUGGESTIONS FOR FURTHER READING

NONFICTION:

Gardner, Richard. THE BOYS AND GIRLS BOOK ABOUT DIVORCE. New York: Bantam, 1970
Gardner, Richard. THE BOYS AND GIRLS BOOK ABOUT ONE-PARENT FAMILIES. New York: G. P. Putnam, 1978
LeShan, Eda. WHAT'S GOING TO HAPPEN TO ME? WHEN PARENTS SEPARATE OR DIVORCE. New York: Four Winds, 1978
Richards, Arlene and Irene Willis. HOW TO GET IT TOGETHER WHEN YOUR PARENTS ARE COMING APART. New York: David McKay, 1976

FICTION*:

Intermediate Level

Agel, Nan Hayden. SUSAN'S MAGIC. New York: Clarion Books, 1973

Alexander, Anne. TO LIVE A LIE. New York: Atheneum, 1975

Anker, Charlotte. LAST NIGHT I SAW ANDROMEDA. New York: Walch, 1975

Blue, Rose. A MONTH OF SUNDAYS. New York: Franklin Watts, 1972

Blume, Judy. IT'S NOT THE END OF THE WORLD. Scarsdale, New York: Bradbury, 1972

Bradbury, Bianca. BOY ON THE RUN. New York: Clarion Books, 1975

Butterworth, W. E.. STEVE BELLAMY. Boston: Little Brown, 1970

Ewing, Kathryn. A PRIVATE MATTER. New York: Harcourt Brace Jovanovich, 1975

Green, Phyllis. ICE RIVER. Reading, Massachusetts: Addison Wesley, 1975

Greene, Constance. A GIRL CALLED AL. New York: Viking, 1969

Greene, Constance. I KNOW YOU, AL. New York: Viking, 1975

Johnson, Annabel and Edgar. THE GRIZZLY. New York: Harper and Row, 1964

Klein, Norma. MOM, THE WOLF MAN, AND ME. New York: Pantheon, 1972

Klein, Norma. TAKING SIDES. New York: Pantheon, 1974

Klein, Norma. WHAT IT'S ALL ABOUT. New York: Dial, 1975

Mann, Peggy. MY DAD LIVES IN A DOWNTOWN MOTEL. Garden City, New York: Doubleday, 1973

Mazer, Norma. I, TRISSY. New York: Delacorte, 1971

McGraw, Eloise Jarvis. A REALLY WEIRD SUMMER. New York: Atheneum, 1978

McHargue, Georgess. STONEFLIGHT. New York: Viking Press, 1975

Newfield, Marcia. A BOOK FOR JODAN. New York: Atheneum, 1975

Norris, Gunilla. LILLIAN. New York: Atheneum, 1968

Perl, Lila. THE TELLTALE SUMMER OF TINA C. New York: Clarion Books, 1975

Pevsner, Stella. A SMART KID LIKE YOU. New York: Clarion Books, 1975

Sachs, Marilyn. THE BEAR'S HOUSE. New York: Doubleday, 1971

Slote, Alfred. MATT GARGAN'S BOY. Philadelphia: Lippincott, 1975

Snyder, Zilpha Keatley. HEADLESS CUPID. New York: Atheneum, 1971

Stanek, Muriel. I WON'T GO WITHOUT A FATHER. Chicago: Whitman, 1972

Sullivan, Mary. BLUE GRASS IGGY. Nashville: Nelson, 1975

Warren, Mary Phraner. THE HAUNTED KITCHEN. Philadelphia: Westminster Press, 1976

FICTION:*

Young Adult Level

Arundel, Honor. A FAMILY FAILING. Nashville: Nelson, 1972

Bradbury, Bianca. THE BLUE YEAR. New York: Ives Washburn, 1967

Brooks, Jerome. UNCLE MIKE'S BOY. New York: Harper and Row, 1973

Colman, Hila. AFTER THE WEDDING. New York: William Morrow, 1975

Donovan, John. I'LL GET THERE, IT BETTER BE WORTH THE TRIP. New York: Harper and Row, 1969

Eyerly, Jeannette. THE WORLD OF ELLEN MARCH. New York: Lippincott, 1964

Holland, Isabell. HEADS YOU WIN, TAILS I LOSE. New York: Lippincott, 1973

Holland, Isabell. OF LOVE AND DEATH AND OTHER JOURNEYS. New York: Lippincott, 1975

Hunter, Evan. ME AND MR. STENNER. New York: Lippincott, 1976

Mazer, Harry. GUY LENNY. New York: Delacorte Press, 1971

Naylor, Phyllis. NO EASY CIRCLE. Chicago: Follet, 1972

Neville, Emily Cheney. GARDEN OF BROKEN GLASS. New York: Delacorte, 1975

Pfeffer, Susan Beth. MARLY THE KID. Garden City, New York: Doubleday, 1975

Smith, Doris. KICK A STONE HOME. New York: Crowell, 1974

Stolz, Mary. LOOK BEFORE YOU LEAP. New York: Harper and Row, 1972

Wolitzer, Hilma. OUT OF LOVE. New York: Farrar, Straus & Giroux, 1976

SUGGESTED READING FOR PARENTS:

Baruth, Leroy G. A SINGLE PARENT'S SURVIVAL GUIDE: HOW TO RAISE THE CHILDREN. Dubuque, Iowa: Kendall Hunt, 1979

Capaldi, Frederick and Barbara McRae. STEP-FAMILIES. New York: Franklin Watts, 1979

Gardner, Richard. THE PARENTS' BOOK ABOUT DIVORCE. Garden City, New York: Doubleday, 1977

Gettleman, Susan and Janet Markowitz. THE COURAGE TO DIVORCE. New York: Simon and Schuster, 1974

Grollman, Earl. TALKING ABOUT DIVORCE: A DIALOGUE BETWEEN PARENT AND CHILD. Boston: Beacon Press, 1975

Krantzler, Mel. CREATIVE DIVORCE. New York: M. Evans, 1974

Levine, James. WHO WILL RAISE THE CHILDREN? New York: Lippincott, 1976

Noble, June and William. HOW TO LIVE WITH OTHER PEOPLE'S CHILDREN. New York: Hawthorn Books, 1977

Peterson, James and Michael Brily. WIDOWS AND WIDOWHOOD. New York: Association Press, 1977

Ramos, Suzanne. THE COMPLETE BOOK OF CHILD CUSTODY. New York: G. P. Putnam, 1979

Roman, Mel and William Haddad. THE DISPOSABLE PARENT: THE CASE FOR JOINT CUSTODY. New York: G. P. Putnam, 1979

Roosevelt, Ruth and Jeannette Lofas. LIVING IN STEP. New York: McGraw-Hill, 1976

Salk, Lee. WHAT EVERY CHILD WOULD LIKE PARENTS TO KNOW ABOUT DIVORCE. New York: Harper and Row, 1978

Satir, Virginia. PEOPLEMAKING. Palo Alto, California: Science and Behavior Books, 1972

Weiss, Robert S. GOING IT ALONE: THE FAMILY LIFE AND SOCIAL SITUATION OF THE SINGLE PARENT. New York: Basic Books, 1979

Weiss, Robert S. MARITAL SEPARATION. New York: Basic Books, 1975

*The author wishes to thank Kathy Nielson of the Fletcher Free Library, Burlington, Vermont, and the Information Center of Parents Without Partners for help in compiling this list.

INDEX